This is NO Adventure Story!

Written by Zoë Clarke

Illustrated by Alankrita Amaya

Sanjay and Sunny were on a walk.
Sanjay was collecting things for the school science table.
Sunny was not. "I'm going on an adventure!"
Sanjay frowned. "This is not an adventure story."

Just then, Sunny saw a piece of paper folded up inside a tree stump. He wrestled it free. "Are you sure? This looks like a treasure map to me!"

"We need to find something to help us on our adventure," Sunny said. "Like our bicycles." Sunny jostled the tree branches aside to free their bicycles and helmets. "Come on!"

Sanjay jumped on to his bicycle and followed
Sunny. "This is not a bicycle adventure story."
Sunny grinned. "Are you sure? We're on bicycles,
and we're off on an adventure!"

Sunny stopped. "Hmm. What we need is a clue."
There was a postcard nestling in a hedge. "Look!
It's a picture clue. I wish I had some scissors …"

Sanjay rolled his eyes. "This is not a picture bicycle adventure story."

Sunny held up the picture and the treasure map. "Are you sure? This path matches the treasure map!"

"Now we need to capture a mystery creature that will help us," Sunny said. "I can see the creature now!"

Sanjay blinked. "That is a crow, not a mystery creature."

"This is not a mystery creature picture bicycle adventure story," Sanjay said.

The crow grabbed the picture and flew off.

"Are you sure about that?" Sunny asked.

"Follow that creature!"

"The creature will lead us to the treasure!"
Sunny laughed.

"IT IS A CROW," Sanjay grumbled.

The creature landed in a nest. There was a
mixture of things in there.

Sanjay crossed his arms. "This is not a treasure mystery creature picture bicycle adventure story."
"Are you sure about that?" Sunny asked.
"There's an unusual crystal in the nest!"

They got back on to their bicycles. Sunny held
on to the unusual crystal. Sanjay waved the
treasure map and the picture.
"I bet there's a ruined castle around here,"
Sunny said.

Sanjay was fed up. "This is not a castle treasure mystery creature picture bicycle adventure story!" "You forgot 'crystal'," Sunny said. "And it's 'unusual'."

Sanjay gave him a look.

They pedalled over a hill. "Sanjay, look!"
Sunny pointed ahead.

"Don't tell me," Sanjay said. "You can see
a castle. Does it look full of mystery and
adventure?"

Sunny paused. "Well, yes."

"This is not a castle treasure mystery creature picture bicycle adventure story," Sanjay mumbled. "With an unusual crystal!"
"Are you sure about that?" Sunny asked.
"Here we are ... at a ruined castle!"

"Can you hear a strange sound?" Sunny asked.
Sanjay listened. "That's Dad, whistling.
He's meeting us here."
"I can show him the treasure map, picture
and the unusual crystal!" Sunny said.

They sat in the castle ruins and had a picnic.
Sunny told Dad about their adventure. The
mystery creature joined them.
"You DO know it's just a crow?" Sanjay said.
Sunny grinned.

"What about the school science table?" Sanjay asked sadly.

Sunny opened his bag. "Well, I picked up these things for you when we were on our adventure!"

These are the things Sunny found.

bark from the tree
with the treasure map

twigs and flowers
from the hedge
with the picture

feathers from the
mystery creature's nest

cobwebs from
the ruined castle

"Thank you," Sanjay said.

Sunny smiled. "That's ok."

"So, we got nature things for the school science table AND we had an adventure. This IS an adventure story!" Sanjay said.

"Yes!" Sunny laughed.

Sanjay looked at Sunny. "If you're going on another castle treasure unusual crystal mystery creature picture bicycle adventure in the future …"

"Yes?" Sunny said.

Sanjay grinned. "… I will come, too!"

Phonics Practice

Say the sound and read the words.

/ch+u/	-ture

picture   adventure   creature   future
nature   capture

/i/	-y

mystery   mysterious   crystal   bicycle
cygnet   gymnast

/s/	sc

scissors   scene   scent   science   scientist

Can you say your own sentences using some of the words on these pages?

What other words do you know that are spelled in these ways?

/s/	-st-

wrestled   rustling   listen   jostled

castle   whistle

Common exception words

thought   through   laughed   many

who   again

We may say some words differently because of our accent.

Talk about the story

Answer the questions:

1 Where did Sunny find the treasure map?

2 What did the boys find inside the bird's nest?

3 Why do you think Sanjay gave Sunny 'a look' on page 13?

4 What was Dad doing while the boys were having an adventure?

5 Have you ever followed a map like the boys in the story? What happened?

6 What kind of adventure stories do you like?

Can you retell the story in your own words?